Write Short to Succeed:

Hows and Whys of Writing Short Stories and Articles

Conda V. Douglas

Write Short to Succeed:
Hows and Whys of Writing Short Stories and Articles

Copyright © 2015 by Conda V. Douglas

All rights reserved.

No part of this book may be reproduced or transmitted in any form or by any means without written permission from the author.

Cover by: Bruce Demaree

ISBN: 978-1-62206-051-1

Dedication: To my good friend, excellent editor and awesome author, Kathy McIntosh.

Table of Contents:

		page
	A Short Introduction, Of Course!	i
	How to Use Write Short to Succeed: One Short Word: Play	ii

SECTION ONE: THE WHYS

1	Because it's a free class in editing and writing	1
2	Because it's easy and fast to learn different ways to write	3
3	Because you can use short writing as exercises to apply what you've learned elsewhere	5
4	Because you can learn how to write better drafts, even first drafts	7
5	Because it teaches you how to write tight and clean right from the first word to the last	10
6	Because it's great for learning about any subject	12
7	Because you finish a piece of writing	14
8	Because you learn how to find and submit to markets	15
9	Because you learn how to survive rejection and then thrive from rejection	17
10	Because short stories can become the inspiration and basis for novels and vice versa	19
11	Because it keeps your writing style more current, with part of today's writing world	21
12	Because publishers love published authors	23
13	Because a short story or collection of short stories can be very useful for promotion and "branding an author"	25
14	Because it's a great way to break writer's block	27

SECTION TWO: THE HOWS OF WRITING SHORT

15 READ and read short stories and articles — 29

16 Let's presume to talk about premises and hypotheses — 31

17 Guidelines for writing short — 35

18 Tips, hints and exercises to get you started — 40

19 Write a short story or article or anything short a week or every two weeks — 42

20 Keep files of ideas — 44

21 Play the title game — 46

SECTION THREE: WHERE AND HOW TO SELL (MARKETS)

22 A-marketing we go — 48

23 Getting paid — 50

24 It's a contest — 53

25 And last, you can consider self-publishing — 56

26 A bonus example of what else you can do with writing short, a story *and* a recipe — 59

27 Just for fun … and a request — 63

Conda V. Douglas Bio and Links — 65

A Short Introduction, Of Course!

Thank you for buying and welcome to *Write Short to Succeed*.

Writing short is a useful, easy to learn, path to a successful writing career. In these pages you'll find numerous tips, secrets, ways and suggestions for how to write short that will have you writing in no time with little effort.

Because I write short, I've succeeded in being a well-published award winning author.

In my writing career, I've published over 100 short stories and articles and have two novel series out. I've been an editor of several magazines and newsletters. For four years, I was a publisher and editor of genre fiction in Ebook format.

All of this began with my writing short.

Writing short has always provided a wealth of information about writing itself.

Without it, I'd never have known that truly I needed to write what I knew. I'm a fifth generation Idahoan and boy, do I know Idaho! Myriad short stories and articles with settings, characters and about my beloved state proved that I'm one of the lucky few who do.

For more about me, visit my blog, *Conda's Creative Center*, and discover lots of writing tips, plus other ways to be creative, and recipes: http://condascreativecenter.blogspot.com.

For some of my publications visit my author page on Amazon: https://www.amazon.com/author/condadouglas.

How to Use *Write Short to Succeed*

One Short Word:
Play

There is one main way that you will find these pages to be most useful: remember to play while doing the exercises or writing from inspiration from the chapters.

Although I'm using the words "work" and "exercises" it's not in a punitive way … perhaps it's best to think of this book as chock-a-block full of "home play."

One of the best things about writing short is that you can relax and play around with every suggestion, chapter and exercise here. In fact, playing with the exercises often creates inspiration.

So play away!

This workbook is set out in three sections.

Section One is about the reasons for writing short, with exercises that will get you started immediately on improving your writing.

Section Two is about how to write short, again with exercises so that you are creating short stories and articles right away.

The last section, *Three*, is about markets and marketing, with exercises that will help you find markets and decide whether to sell your work or self-publish.

Since the workbook is laid out as a class in writing short it is most beneficial to start at the beginning and do all the exercises in order. If you struggle with getting started in the first section then check out a couple of chapters in *Section Two: The Hows* for tips and hints.

If you are like me and prone to jump to the section that most interests you and sometimes skip the exercises, because, hey, exercise can be hard, that will work also. Although I promise these are easy and often fun exercises.

If you are a skipper and jumper, it'll be useful to keep track of what you have read and what exercises you've done to make sure you get them all.

SECTION ONE

The Whys

Chapter One

Because it's a free class in editing and writing

Writing short is an excellent way to learn to write fiction and nonfiction.

Every short story and article must be ... short. Which means you can focus on all the elements of fiction or nonfiction, plot, description, characterization, the five senses and how, who, what and where.

You can experiment and play with different genres, ideas, formats, without committing to hundreds of pages of writing a novel or a nonfiction book before realizing something doesn't work. And most of the time it does work and gives you a finished short story to sell.

Try different genres, characters, try writing the same plot different ways.

It's a writing course you'll get paid for!

Exercise One:

> *Remember: if you need help getting started use* Section Two: The Hows *chapters for tips and hints.*

Write a short piece in some genre or format that you've never written before.

- Always write nonfiction? Then try a short story. If you always write nonfiction, you will discover that writing short stories will add layers to your work.
- Always write nonfiction about the same subject? Try writing an article about something you'd never think of writing about.

- Same is true of writing articles if you are a fiction writer, then try writing an article or essay.
- Always write in the mystery genre? Try horror. Or romance. Step outside that comfortable writing box and learn to write with more skill and acuity.

You'll find that you will be adding color and depth to your nonfiction and better structure and organization to your fiction.

Exercise Two:

Take a short piece of your writing and check to see if you have the elements of good writing within the piece.

If you have never written short before and need some ways to start, no worries, *Section Two: The Hows* is full of tips, secrets, ideas, exercises that will have you writing short in no time.

- For example, for this exercise, does your piece have the five senses? Or at least a couple of the senses, particularly sight and smell, two strong senses that can make a piece come alive. This counts for nonfiction, as well.
- Does it have the who, what, how, why and where? This too counts with both nonfiction and fiction.
- What is the conflict in the piece? Do you have a vivid setting, created in just a few words? Do the characters in the piece come alive and appear distinct from each other?

Play with adding elements and seeing if they strengthen or weaken a piece. The operative word here is *play*.

Chapter Two

Because it's easy and fast to learn different ways to write

When you write short stories and articles you can try a wide, wide variety of different ways to write. Play with your manuscripts. Try different approaches — first person then third, perhaps, or start the story at different spots. Many new writers start a story too early, with back story.

With an article try different approaches and a different focus. With a short manuscript if it doesn't work, it's easy to rewrite.

Exercise One:

Take a famous short story and if it's first person, rewrite it as third or second or even omniscient narrator.

If this seems daunting at first, then write a short synopsis of the story, or perhaps an article about the story. Writing synopses of others' work will make it easier to write one of your own. A synopsis is often required when submitting to a publisher.

Exercise Two:

Take a short article from a well-known magazine or newspaper and rewrite it, changing the approach and/or focus of the article.

- Try the type of article that interests you first, and if that is too difficult, look for something you don't care about, because that will give you a touch more objectivity while doing the exercises.

- Look for other angles that might be of interest to a reader and try those.
- Ask: what might be missing from the article? What might be trimmed as it is repetitious or doesn't add enough to the work?

Please note:

With these exercises you are changing the author's words. However, it would still be plagiarism of the author's work if you tried to sell/publish your results.

If you find yourself using this exercise for inspiration to write something completely new and different that's great and one way to start writing short.

Chapter Three

Because you can use short writing as exercises to apply what you've learned elsewhere

Again, writing short means it's short enough to learn how to have an editor's eye. You can go over a short manuscript several times, searching for missing punctuation, for clumsy sentences and for grammar errors.

You can apply what you've learned from classes, critique partners and other writings.

For example, search for passive verbs, too long sentences and run on sentences in your manuscript.

Notice patterns of repetition—do you always start your sentences in a certain way? Do you use passive voice (was, has, had, had been) too often? Are certain words favorites that you use over and over? "Just" and "always" happen to be a couple of mine.

Search for those pesky modifying adverbs. These sneak in everywhere but almost always don't add meaning and often weaken a verb. Let the verb stand on its own.

"He ran" is far better than "he ran quickly." After all, how often does someone run slowly?

<u>Exercise:</u>

Use the "Find" in the Editing tab of your Word doc to search for those too common words and punctuation.

- For example, exclamation points should be few and far between—or even nonexistent. Let the words themselves show emphasis.
- In fact if there are no exclamation points, all the better! You can see I have a problem with exclamation points ...

- What are your weaknesses? Do you use certain words too often? How about punctuation? Keep a list of those that you overuse.
- If you use passive voice a lot, keep a thesaurus handy. The Word program has a simple one in the "Review" tab.
- Not only use a thesaurus, but also often look up words on online dictionaries. You'll expand your vocabulary and mind that way.

For example "he was running" can become "he ran" but also "he raced," "he sprinted," "he dashed," and it can jog on and on.

Note: many times "he ran" is the best choice as it is simple, straightforward and active. "He darted, he raced, he sprinted," etc. can become intrusive quickly. Use synonyms when he's doing an awful lot of running.

Chapter Four

Because you can learn how to write better drafts, even first drafts

The caveat to learning how to write better drafts, even first drafts, is allowing a first draft to be exactly that: a first draft.

What that means is to train yourself to "kill the editor" while writing the very first draft. It's meant to be rough, so write it as quickly as you can.

Ignore whether you are overusing punctuation, certain words and/or not using the five senses or who, what, where and when. That's for later drafts when you revive the dead editor.

Writing the first draft quickly without the editor trains our writer brains to subconsciously apply the lessons learned about writing.

Once you have that rough first draft completed, then it's time to rewrite. It's best not to "anticipate" and start your editing before the draft is finished. Otherwise you'll be tempted, once you see the rough draft errors, to start the draft over again. And again. And again. No!

Rewriting a twenty page short story or article draft is a lot less intimidating than rewriting three hundred. Plus, you can rewrite a short piece several times if you wish, learning as you go.

The same holds true for editing your writing. Again, editing twenty pages is a lot less daunting than editing three hundred. Doing a final "tweak" or fine line edit on twenty pages is a lot less unnerving than tweaking three hundred pages. (By "tweak" or fine line edit I mean is the grammar and punctuation there and correct? Is every word spelled correctly? Did you use the correct word — too or to or two, etc.?)

Because you can rewrite, edit, and tweak a short piece several times quickly, you'll learn what your strengths and weaknesses are. It's the best way to learn: by doing. Then you can consciously avoid flaws, sticking points and no-no's, even in first drafts. You will consciously and then over time and with practice subconsciously write to your strengths.

For example, nowadays in my first draft I'm much more likely to add the five senses to every scene of my fiction—or at least two or three. I know I use too many exclamation points but since I am aware when I use them I use far, far fewer to begin with. I know the sentence patterns that I repeat too often and will catch myself doing same—in a first rough draft. My first drafts are now much more like my third drafts used to be.

There's one more advantage of writing short to learn how to write first drafts well. Copy and line editors get paid money to edit. It's quite expensive for three hundred pages. However, you can send a well-written-and-edited-by-you short story or article to an editor without going broke. This is a way to avoid paying the editor to provide missing periods, misspelled words, and other simple first draft edits. An objective edit from an editor can teach you a lot about your writing.

Exercise:

> *Remember: if you need help getting started visit* Section Two: The Hows *chapters.*

Set a timer for ten minutes.

Use an oven timer or your phone. If using your phone put it someplace you can't see the screen "ticking down." If you're using an old-fashioned timer that ticks put it somewhere you can't see it or hear it ticking, but can hear it ring after ten minutes. This prevents you from watching/listening to the timer instead of writing.

Pick a short piece to write for a rough first draft.

Turn on the timer.

Write!

- Try to beat the clock and finish the piece or at least 3-4 pages of the draft before the timer goes off. It's a race that will "kill the editor" for those ten minutes.
- You can write the entire piece in three or four ten minute increments that way, as an exercise. You might be quite pleased at the resulting first draft.
- If not, then simply try again. And again. Remember that the more you write the better you'll be.

Chapter Five

Because it teaches you how to write tight and clean right from the first word to the last

This is one of the major benefits of writing short.

What constitutes a good or great read has changed considerably in the last few years as readers, along with everyone else, are now participating in the fast paced digital age. We've gotten used to lots of meaning in a few words — think texting.

Readers are now drawn to reads with a great deal of "white space" on the page. That means short sentences and short blocks of text. Look at *Write Short to Succeed*.

We've become a world of scan readers.

That means a writer needs to make every word count and every word work on several different levels. Writing short teaches a writer how to write tight, necessary if you're writing a one page essay or flash fiction or a 400 page novel or treatise.

For example, compare a piece of Victorian writing to a comparable piece of modern, within the last 15 years, writing. Comparable means fiction to fiction and nonfiction to nonfiction.

Exercise:

Take a piece of published writing, not your own, a fairly lengthy article or short story, at least a thousand words, but no more than twenty-five hundred. Edit it to make it as short as possible.

- What words can be cut without a loss of meaning? Can paragraphs be combined? Are things stated several times when once, twice or thrice would be sufficient?
- Then consider the results of your edits.

- Does the piece work better? Is it an easier read? If not, why not? If not, usually the answer is that you've cut too much, leading to confusion.

Chapter Six

Because it's great for learning about any subject

If you are doing research on something, a place, or a culture, or a condition or a process, write an article about it, or write a short story that contains the information. The old saying that *if you want to learn a subject well then teach about it*, is true.

Write a short story about something new. Or an article.

At the very least, writing a narrative will clarify the subject and make clear the gaps around what you're researching.

This is useful even if you know the subject well.

For example, I grew up in an art gallery with a dad who was an artist and a jewelry designer. I, too, made, and still make, my own jewelry. The main character in my cozy mystery *Starke Dead* series is a jewelry designer.

I discovered when I wrote articles about jewelry making that there was sometimes too little information in my novels about the different processes and sometimes too much. Writing articles about the jewelry making taught me what to add to my fiction that would clarify the process.

When I'd included too much information within a work the articles helped me to condense and trim the information while still having it clear and concise.

Exercise One:

Pick a subject, or issue, or anything you'd like to know more about, research it briefly and write an article about it.

Or write a short story using the subject as a setting, or central theme or plot device.

Exercise Two:

What other ways could you find to use a short piece to learn how to do, well, anything?

Play with this one.

Make a silly, out-there list.

Mine has "scaling a skyscraper" on it, which has turned out to be quite useful information. One of the fairies in my *Mall Fairies* series has only one wing and therefore has to climb fairy-sized "skyscrapers," a flight of stairs, big rocks, etc.

Chapter Seven

Because you finish a piece of writing

There's a great deal of power in writing the word "End." Completing a writing project carries with it a great deal of satisfaction.

However, many authors have the dreaded one to three chapters of several novels stuffed in a drawer, because the writer couldn't face writing another couple of hundred pages.

Writing short and finishing short pieces gives you confidence and the knowledge you can create an entire story, plot, characterization, etc. start to finish.

Plus, after you've written a few short stories, it's easier to imagine writing many, many more pages—perhaps even a novel or full length nonfiction book.

There's another element to being able to finish a short piece.

If it is a short piece the excuses for not writing the entire thing tend to evaporate or at the very least become absurd. Can't face writing 3,000 words, a whole 10 pages? How about 2,000, or 1,500, or even a 1,000 word story or article?

Actually, the last, something 1,000 or less words start to finish, can be the most difficult to write. It can be hard to "squeeze in" enough elements of a short story or article into three pages or less. There is more about this in *Section Two: The Hows*.

Don't have time to write a longer work? How about a shorter one?

It's true that your first attempts at writing short may take you a little while. But if you play with the exercises in this book you'll find that pretty quickly you're writing and finishing multiple works.

Chapter Eight

Because you learn how to find and submit to markets

You learn how to easily find many markets for your work and then how to write a query, and/or format a piece for submission according to the different requirements of each market.

As a major added plus, you will learn how to gauge a market's suitability for your work. It's more than merely finding a magazine or anthology that takes the length and subject or genre of your manuscript.

Finding a fit for your piece is a subjective thing.

For example, a magazine that takes horror may take a wide selection of stories that stretch the definition of horror or only traditional ghost stories or only vampire stories or any number of different variations.

This is the sort of thing that can only be learned by doing, a number of times.

You also learn how to judge different markets. There are some that you may want to write a piece specifically for. There are some you won't want to submit to at all.

Hint, it's not always about the money, although money is always a consideration as I will talk about in *Section Three: Where and How to Sell*.

Exercise:

Be a critical reader.

> *By that I mean that when you are reading any short writing piece, whether it is fiction or nonfiction, read the piece with an author's eye to submission.*

- Read to see if *your* work would be a fit or a misfit.

- Why and how does the piece fit within the publication? Or does it?

I suspect that many of you have read something in a magazine or anthology and wondered, "Why is this in here?"

Try to answer that question, for you may find that there really isn't an answer. A great lesson in the ultra-subjectivity of acceptance and rejection, which brings us to the next chapter ...

Chapter Nine

Because you learn how to survive rejection and then thrive from rejection

This is one of the most important things you learn from writing short.

If you write and submit a number of stories and articles, being rejected gets easier. Still stings, but there is less invested in every rejection because you have written and can have several stories out at once.

You'll learn to be a better writer from rejections as well.

Editors will sometimes mention why your piece was returned. Often it's a helpful critique of your work.

I've had many times when I read a rejection, after I got over the sting, where I had an "aha" moment of why the piece needed this or that to be greatly improved. Then after I applied the editor's critiques the piece almost always went on to sell, although not necessarily to that publication.

Other times you will find yourself scratching your writer's mind over a rejection. What, exactly, does the editor mean in the rejection letter? Hunh, what is the editor saying? Refrain from writing the editor back and asking/demanding clarification.

This is where you learn to critique rejection letters.

Since writing is a subjective craft sometimes the editors are wrong. Ask yourself if you can find a way to understand the editor's words. If you consider them and find them lacking then it's most likely that the rejection is too subjective. It can be the case the editor is complaining about something that another editor would love.

Learning to recognize when this is true and when it isn't is one of the reasons writing short will help you succeed in all your writing endeavors.

And of course, there is always that acceptance which spurs you on.

Once you have that acceptance, you learn how to go through the sometimes difficult process of editing. You learn what edits to accept and which to reject and why, simply by going through the process several times.

Exercise:

Write your own rejection slips.

- Play with this, have fun. I know, you're saying "Play with something so painful as a rejection?"
- What you will find is that the more extreme you can write the letter the more you can receive and accept real rejection letters.
- It's a practice being rejected. Overall, editors will be much kinder than any rejection letter that you write to yourself.
- It's also a practice in writing short. Writing short is exactly that, whether a letter or short story or article.

Here's my over-the-top rejection letter to get you started:

Dear Will-Never-Be-A-Real-Author,

I have received and read your hideous, vile submission.

Ugh. I had a bout of projectile vomiting during the reading, but managed to get through the whole 100 words.

However, this has left me unable to go on as an editor. This is my last rejection as I'm leaving soon for the asylum.

I beg of you, please, never write again.

Sincerely,

Suicidal Editor

Chapter Ten

Because short stories can become the inspiration and basis for novels and vice versa

All of my series have come from short stories.

My *Mall Fairies* series began as a short story of only 3,000 words. But the characters kept nagging me to tell more about them and their world. The short story kept getting longer and longer, with more and more ideas, characters, plot and complex setting occurring to me with every draft.

This is another benefit to writing short, it can tell you whether you have enough material for a short story or a novella or a novel or even, as in my case an entire trilogy and series.

Or not.

Sometimes the characters, plot, etc. will only support a short story. And sometimes the short format *enhances* the characters, plot, etc.

I've often "pulled" a character from one of my novels and had that character "star" in his or her own short story. This has also led to inspiration for my next novel in that series.

Writing short stories about characters is also a wonderful way to develop a character.

There are other benefits, not so inspirational, that come from writing short.

If you write something short that never works no matter how hard you work on it you can throw it away. Yes, I said *throw it away*. Consider it a learning lesson and move on. Or cannibalize it for the good elements and write something new.

I've done this, cannibalizing, with my first "drawer" novel. A drawer novel is the first one, where new novelists learn how *not* to write a novel. Mine is resting someplace where hopefully no one finds it after I die.

But I keep the drawer novel around to take bits and pieces and write short stories. Which I did for my short story, *Blink of An Eye*, which years ago sold to a magazine. Now the story is only available reprinted in my anthology *Mild West Mysteries*.

So in a sense, I'm making money off my first novel!

Exercise:

Do you have an idea for a piece of writing? A compelling character for fiction, perhaps? Or a subject matter that speaks to you for nonfiction? Or an event that could be either?

Write a short piece to get a feel for "how much" material you might truly have.

It could be a short piece or a chapter in a longer work or the main character for a novel. Or it could be the synopsis for a longer work.

Chapter Eleven

Because it keeps your writing style more current, with part of today's writing world

This is a subtle but valuable benefit.

It can take years to write a novel or nonfiction book. Writing something short will take … much shorter. Occasionally writing a short story or article, finding markets and sending it out there will keep a writer knowledgeable about our rapidly changing writing world.

The writing world is one of fashion and shifting tastes.

Perhaps the most glaring change in our reading and therefore writing is that we now love "white space." White space means that readers are drawn to short sentences and short paragraphs so that there is a lot of white instead of text on the page.

Big blocks of text drive readers away.

If you compare a Victorian novel to a modern novel, the difference is obvious. Or compare this book, *Write Short to Succeed*, to a nonfiction book on writing from, say, the 1950s. Or if you remember an English Lit class in high school or college and reading the classics you'll understand our love of white space.

Even grammar goes in and out of fashion.

The Oxford comma, for example, is currently out of fashion. So are semicolons. Will they come back in? Who knows?

All sorts of writerly things change all the time and one way to keep up and keep in style is to write short.

Exercise:

Take a short story or article from the eighteenth or nineteenth century and rewrite it using contemporary language and style.

Mark Twain's short stories or essays, or *A Modest Proposal* by Jonathan Swift, or Edgar Allen Poe's short stories, or *Civil Disobedience* by Henry David Thoreau, or something by Charles Dickens will work. Or if you still have your old school English Lit textbook, use that.

If you struggle with rewriting the all too familiar classics, go to Amazon and type in things like "nineteenth century short stories" and a number of selections will come up for you to consider. Some of these authors may be available at your local library.

- For this exercise find something in your particular genre.
- If you do this exercise as a way to understand how language shifts and changes like the living thing that it is, then don't consider publishing your results. With just language changes, your work will be too close to the original.
- If, however, you find that you take an inspiration from the short story or article and riff off of it in a new direction so that it is entirely different feel free to consider publication.

Chapter Twelve

Because publishers love published authors

When a publisher receives a submission from an author who has published before, the publisher knows that particular author has been through the entire process, from writing to editing to selling, editing again and publishing.

Publishers know those authors know about the business, know about having a writing career, know what it means to promote and have been through the different steps in the process of being published.

A minor advantage is that editors can be neurotic too, just like writers. So they love that someone else has vetted you as an author and determined that "this author is good."

Not fair perhaps, but also perhaps human nature.

Writing short means that you have many opportunities to publish in a wide variety of publications.

It takes less time to write a short piece than an entire book.

Having anything on your resume, although most publishers will accept submissions from a "pre-published" writer, is a gold star on your forehead that shouts "I'm a pro!"

One of the best things about the advent of Ebooks is that publishers no longer insist, if that particular publisher ever did insist, on being published within the genre of their publications.

In other words romance writers could only use their *romance* publications on their resume. Breaking into a genre where you hadn't published before was difficult.

Ebooks have changed all of that, with publishers realizing through the great stuff self-published that writers who can write, can write. Who knew?

There are some exceptions to the "published before" status especially in regards to self-published short stories and articles. This is because there are so many self-published authors now. It's difficult for a self-published author to stand out from this pack of millions.

There is a way this can happen. If it becomes a noticeable success and therefore stands out from the sheer vast array of self-published material. If the short work sells many, many copies or goes viral in some way then that's different.

Such success with a self-publication only rarely happens. While it's delightful when it does, there's no way to predict when it will.

However, that doesn't mean you should never self-publish anything. There is more on this in *Section Three: Where and How to Sell.*

Chapter Thirteen

Because a short story or collection of short stories can be very useful for promotion and "branding an author"

There are several ways to use short stories for promotion and branding.

One is the traditional way of selling and publishing in magazines and anthologies. The major promotional benefit comes from *being* in a magazine, anthology or collection.

The publishers will, of course, heavily *promote* your writing since they wish to sell their product to as many readers as possible. As well, most publishers will work with you to promote the publication, whether it be a magazine or anthology. Their work with you can be a useful and informative course in how to promote all your work.

Also, there is usually a lot of cross-promotion between the different authors within a magazine, anthology or collection.

This is the main benefit, in many ways, to selling your short work to a publisher or publication.

There are also large, if secondary benefits, to selling short stories and articles to magazines and anthologies.

First, the publishers will professionally edit and produce your piece. Working with professional editors means you learn better how to edit your pieces yourself. This is useful for better submissions and also for when you self-publish to promote.

The publishers also do the cover of the publication, format for the different publication instruments, whether Ebook or print or both, all the while working hard to produce the best product possible. This is another useful "class" in promotion, this one about producing a saleable product.

Plus publishers will pay you for your work. (There's a discussion on unpaid markets and whether or not you should submit to them in *Section Three*. Never pay a publisher or publication to publish your work.)

Once you're a professional, i.e., paid author, you can use that in your promotional materials. You can also submit to legitimate contests, which if you win, will add to your promotion. Publishers submit collections to contests as well. If the collection or anthology wins, so do you! A line such as: "author in the award winning anthology …" is a powerful piece of promotion.

Which brings me to a caveat: Always check to see what rights you are selling. If the magazine or anthology takes right of first publication, it means the piece must be never before published and the publication will not buy reprints. Most buy *one time publication rights*. There is quite a bit more about rights in *Section Three: Where and How to Sell*.

Exercise:

Go over your writings with these questions in mind:

- What do I often focus on or write a lot about in my writings?
- What in my writings is different from most other author's writings? Example: I write about Idaho.
- What am I writing about that speaks most to my heart? I love my home state of Idaho and the people who live here.

Chapter Fourteen

Because it's a great way to break writer's block

Ah, the bane of a writer's existence, the dreaded and dreadful writer's block. Who hasn't faced that terror of all terrors: a blank page?

No worries, help is at hand.

First of all, so many times what blocks us is the overwhelm of the responsibility of putting many words on many pages. This is more difficult when facing a book length work.

Writing short is ... short writing. Easier to imagine doing and finishing.

Motivational speakers talk about the "power move," of positivity, an action you take that changes your mind-set from negative or in a rut to positive and often stimulates creativity. Writing short when you normally write long can have a similar effect, as can changing genres, first person to third, etc.

Exercise:

If you are facing a blank page and a panicked mind use this book to break your blocks.

- Scan through the exercises in *Section One* and *Section Two* and pick one that seems easy — or if not easy at least not painful.
- Remember that these are exercises that are meant to get you playing with your writing and succeeding.
- There is no right or wrong way to play with the exercises, just write. If one exercise doesn't quite break the block, simply try another.

SECTION TWO

The Hows of Writing Short

Chapter Fifteen

READ and read short stories and articles

The major way to learn how to write short stories: *read* short stories, articles, essays, collections and anthologies of any type.

Read a lot, they're short, after all. Read stories in publications you want to be in. Read a lot in your genre, but not exclusively so.

Read magazines, book collections, and published standalones. Read the classics and the brand new releases and everything in between.

Much of the time, unless you know the author and know they write well, I would suggest not reading self-published works because there is no knowing the quality of the work.

There are of course exceptions, always. If a self-published work has a number of four and five star reviews then go ahead and read.

And of course, there is an exception to an exception.

From time to time you might want to read … um, look at, something self-published or even published by a publisher that has nothing but terrible reviews.

Why? Because sometimes the worst writing can teach you a lot about writing better.

Exercise:

Find a wide variety of short writings to read.

- It's not necessary to spend a lot, or a little, or even any money to do so. Your local library will have a wealth of titles to choose from.
- Read articles on the internet. Many newspapers and magazines have free content.

- Amazon also has a wide variety of short writings available on Ebook.

On Amazon, if you search on the books tab for a genre, say short stories, and then select "Price: low to high" on the drop down menu, you'll find a number of free selections first. This is the time to read reviews to see if the work is worth downloading, however, remember that the free reads are just that—FREE.

Chapter Sixteen

Let's presume to talk about premises and hypotheses

For fiction, you'll find that premises can be very useful. A premise can keep your writing on track.

What is a fiction premise? It's not the plot, theme or even idea; it's all of those elements and often a moral conundrum.

A premise is an author's statement made by the events, characters, and conclusion of a story. The statement may be a widely accepted truth, or go against a widely accepted truth. The conflict of the story will be within the premise.

A way to build a story from a premise could be starting with a statement such as: "Work hard and you'll succeed." Then play a "What if?" game.

What if the main character can't get a job? Any work? What then?

What if the main character works extremely hard for years and never succeeds? Fellow authors, I'm sure you can sympathize with that one.

What if the work kills your main character? Talk about a horror story!

Another way to think about premises is as a previously unexplored angle on a familiar subject. You might reach it by twisting a cliché or taking a fresh look at an old subject or plot. Many story premises can be boiled down to a cliché (as above).

A few words of caution here: don't get "trapped" within a premise. Never force a story to fit a premise. Premises are meant to be tools to get you writing and a kind of map for the story. If the premise doesn't work, discard it and try another.

Here's an award winning hundred word flash story of mine as an example.

The cliché here is: If you don't forgive, you can't move on, which leads to all sorts of problems, including death. That's the conflict.

A longer version of this story is in my short story anthology, *Mild West Mysteries*.

HEAD STANDS

Southerner Grandfather MacDonald lost his leg during the Gettysburg battle and ever after wore a wooden peg leg.

Grandpa and his Northerner blind wife carried on an un-Civil war. She stood on her head, believing it'd bring her sight. Grandpa, seeing his wife's head stands, often escaped to the roof.

One day, she popped out of the roof hatch.

He slipped on his peg leg and tumbled off, breaking his fall with his neck. His last words: "I knew that Yankee'd get me some day."

We never did know if he meant his wife or the soldier who shot him.

Like a premise, a hypothesis is useful for keeping your nonfiction on track.

Hypotheses are statements that the article proves.

Eating right is healthy. Scientific studies have shown this. People who eat this way have been proven to be healthier, etc. So here's one way how.

For example, one of my published articles was "Controlling Portions, Controlling Pounds." The article was about one way to be a healthy weight by controlling portions. Using smaller plates to control portion size and what a portion truly was—three ounces of meat is about the size of a deck of cards—were both covered in the article.

Those two subjects were *all* that I wrote about. There's tons more about eating right, but for an article I focused on one narrow topic.

Exercise One:

For fiction, find some clichés such as "the exception proves the rule" and "wish not, want not."

- What are stories that you can hang on such statements? Play the "What if" game as mentioned above.
- You can even twist the statement, for example, "if you wish for it, you'll want it." And what if you'll do anything to get it?

    There's a statement for a mystery story.

Exercise Two:

For nonfiction, find hypotheses that would work for nonfiction such as "exercise to live longer." Then narrow your focus by asking questions.

- What is the audience for this particular subject?
- In most cases an article for a magazine for senior citizens will be a much different focus than for marathon trainees.

- What is a focused subject with your hypothesis that has not been written about many times and in depth?
- For example, much has been written about senior citizens who can't exercise the usual ways due to age and infirmary. So what about those senior citizens that *do* run marathons? What should their fitness regimen be?
- Or how about senior citizens who are very fit, but have minor trouble due to arthritis or age-related injuries, so cannot participate in regular exercise classes. But "senior" classes are too easy and don't challenge the "fit senior."

All examples are twists that give different angles for different articles.

Chapter Seventeen

Guidelines for writing short

For fiction:

A short story can have one major conflict only.

There's simply not room to wedge in even a small subplot. Note: You can sometimes get away with an echo, i.e., the repeat of a situation that echoes the main problem.

The same goes for settings and characters.

If you find yourself struggling with too many settings and/or characters go through the piece and see if you can *combine* same.

For example, what are the elements of a setting that are completely necessary for the short story? Can the story take place in just one setting? Or two? Or at most, three?

Same is true for characters. Plus, check to make sure that each character has more than one function in the short story. This is true with novels as well.

For example, a "best friend to the detective" in a mystery needs to be something more than only a traditional sounding board for the detective. Perhaps a suspect? And/or a love interest? Or their own detective, getting in the way of the main character?

All elements need to create tension/conflict/action.

Exposition is the enemy of writing short.

For example, any description needs to set a mood with some tension and possibly conflict. Ask yourself this when describing anything: why am I describing this? What does it add to the story?

Make sure all dialog is content rich.

Dialog is similar to how we speak, but not the same. Our speech is full of pauses, phrases that have no meaning, and repetitious phrases.

Every word of dialog needs to have meaning. Even a phrase such as "Um …" should show not only hesitation, but something about the character speaking. Is he always hesitant? Or is he thinking up a lie?

Don't explain anything.

Keep in mind to R.U.E, resist the urge to explain. Trust your readers to understand, they're smart readers after all. The information needs to come from the characters, dialog and description.

Do have character tags.

Character tags are actions, attitudes and character appearances that are unique to that character. Voice, including dialects and speech oddities, gestures, including but not limited to nervous tics, clothing and hair, and mental states such as always angry are all character tags.

For examples, Harry Potter has his geeky glasses, Scrooge won't let his assistant off for Christmas and Scooby Doo will do anything for snacks.

In my *Starke Dead* novels I have a Native American character whose Indian name is Running Bear. He's a bear of man who can run just like a bear as in very fast, when he wants to/needs to.

Dora, my main character, always wears her oversize, wax-spattered jeweler's apron. She'll shove her hands into her apron pockets when upset.

Character tags are a useful shorthand when writing short. In a short piece limit your character tags to one or two for each character.

Avoid being anecdotal.

The shorter the piece, the more it's tempting to tell the tale instead of showing the tale, such as "This happened and then this happened and then the end."

Every story needs a beginning, a middle and an end. Plus, most important, a story arc.

Here's one of the best examples of a truly short story, only six words, that is not an anecdote. This story is apocryphally attributed to Hemingway, but actually came from a play about him: "For sale, baby shoes, never worn." See how the reader creates the story?

Do use *** or ### to show major scene breaks or a passage of time.

In a short story there usually isn't space to have chapters or to "set a new scene" or to use a paragraph to describe a passage of time. This is when asterisks or hashtags come in handy.

Like character tags, they are a form of shorthand. Just make sure that you keep the style consistent. Use either hashtags or asterisks, never both. Use the same number of the symbol each time and no more than five asterisks or hashtags.

For nonfiction:

An article or essay can have only one main focus.

For example if you are writing about losing weight, focus on one narrow aspect of successful weight loss, instead of the various problems and issues of obesity.

Asides on related topics to the main article are to be avoided.

Like fiction, every sentence needs to be content rich.

After you write a first draft, consider what each sentence says. Does it say something new and different? If not, you may be not resisting re-stating things, so ...

... Resist re-stating things.

This can be difficult when writing nonfiction as every author wishes to be clear. It's good to write it all down while writing the first draft, but then use your editor's eye to see what can be combined or trimmed.

Do you need to even eliminate some elements of the article or essay because it is too much for a short piece? If so, always remember that eliminated piece may be used for another short nonfiction.

It's useful to return to your hypothesis when editing.

This is when it can be a "road map" to show where you've run off the main highway and down a dirt road.

Exercise One:

Read a fiction story. Start to spot character tags.

- What is unique about this character and how does the author show that? What does the author use: voice, physical actions or attributes, or mental states?
- When and where are the character tags? You'll find that they are whenever a character is introduced.
- How often are the character tags used?

- When reading short stories, count the number of times a character tag is used. You'll notice that in a good short story or even novel it's not all that often. Too many repeats of a character tag gets annoying fast.

Exercise Two:

Read a nonfiction article. See if you can state the hypothesis of the article in one sentence.

- If not, why not?
- How well does the author stick to the hypothesis? Does the author prove the hypothesis?
- Or does the article wander off into side lanes?

For example: "Exercise to get healthier ... oh, and you should eat right too, plus reduce stress ..." The three subjects are closely related, but each is a separate hypothesis.

Chapter Eighteen

Tips, hints and exercises to get you started

Now, let's get you started writing. Here are some suggestions that will help.

Remember to play.

One great way to get started is timed free writing.
Free writing is when you ... write.
Without thought or consideration, just words on a page. Set a timer for five minutes. It's helpful to not be able to see or hear the timer.
Start writing down words. Any words.
"I'm writing, I'm writing, I'm writing," is perfectly acceptable.
Often, you'll find you start writing something that is actual writing. If that happens just keep writing.

Use one of the exercises in *Section One*. For example, try out the one where you rewrite a classic piece. Rewriting other's words can turn off the editor and get you going on your own work.

Find a contest that is themed and see if it inspires you to write a short story or article.
Write a Christmas Letter or a letter to an editor or to a friend or to anyone you wish, whether fictional or real. Tell stories in the letter, or report an event, or give an opinion, or give advice. Even the Christmas Letter can be a total fiction. Hmm, that's given me an idea for a short story ....
Write a Facebook post, or a blog post, or a tweet on twitter or any sort of casual "sharing" media site. Since this is "casual" writing it can be inspiration for "real" writing.

Write a review of a product, service or place on Amazon or Yelp or TripAdvisor. For example, I often write reviews on TripAdvisor. It puts me into "writer" mode.

Exercise One:

For fiction:

Write a story using only dialog.

Write a story using only description.

Write a story using only one character.

The three exercises above are truly writing *exercises*, where you stretch your dialog, description and characterization muscles as it is difficult to write something through just one element.

But they are often quite successful for a short story. At the very least they can be a strong part of a piece.

Exercise Two:

For nonfiction:

Write down ten subjects for articles or essays on small strips of paper. Try to make the subjects diverse but also of interest to you.

For example, for me one subject could be "eating healthy for singles and doubles" and another could be "making polymer clay earrings, should they match?"

- Fold up the strips of paper and toss in a bowl or the more traditional hat. Stir the strips and then pick a piece of paper.
- Start writing on that subject on the paper. Whatever pops into your head. It can be ideas, notes, an outline or synopsis—whatever.
- Trust to the luck of the draw. Take a gamble. Play.

Chapter Nineteen

Write a short story or article or anything short a week or every two weeks

How do you succeed with writing short? Write lots. Like anything, practice makes it better and easier. And the more you write the more you'll reap the benefits mentioned in the chapters above.

Remember to play when you are writing first drafts.

Afterwards they are your babies, which is another advantage to writing lots and lots, because after the first draft you need to turn on the killer editor. Letting the editor rip away at your short piece is much easier if you have many babies and more coming all the time.

The rough drafts are to be worked, reworked and sweated over — briefly.

Then, your short pieces are product. Don't wait to sell a piece before you write another or ten or twenty.

Best yet, do what great short story writer Ray Bradbury always suggested for new authors and write a story a week for a year.

Writing story after story creates the discipline to write. When it becomes a habit, you'll find it's much easier and faster to write short.

Exercise:

Set an intention by keeping a loose schedule of writing goals.

I say "loose" because we writers and other creative types push back against rigidity of any kind. It doesn't set well with our creative minds.

- Instead, the schedule will mean that you "intend" to write this much at these times.
- Try to have goals that are small enough to swallow daily. And then weekly, monthly, etc.
- At first, make the goals smaller than you would want. This is because creative people sometimes expect more of ourselves than is reasonable:

    For example: "I'll write two to three short pieces a day," a new author will cry. And while there are those amazing few who can do this—and my, am I jealous of such authors—most of us would be setting ourselves up for failure.

- After two to three weeks, tweak your intentions as to your experience.

    For example, if you find the goal of writing a short piece a week challenging, set it to one piece every other week.

- Or, if you find writing a short piece a week too easy, set it to two or three pieces a week.

Most of all be gentle with yourself and your writing endeavors.

Chapter Twenty

Keep files of ideas

Even if they don't seem like they are complete or even much of an idea open a new file with each new story.

This encourages your mind to start "filling in the blanks" with an idea, subconsciously developing it.

My extensive notes written down on scraps of envelopes create many of my short stories. Often I'll come up with a plot device, or a character, or a premise and once I write that down more follows.

If you can, write the story or article in a rough draft when inspiration hits. Or at least as much of it as you can.

Remember, this is playtime and all very rough, so keep the editor silent or at least ignore the mutterings of "this is so lame, this will never amount to anything, that's a mixed metaphor, what a cliché, etc."

Write down snatches of conversation, a character that pops into mind, plot and article ideas. These can hit at any time, hence the following exercise.

Exercise:

Go out and buy a cheap notebook. I like the 6" x 9" spiral bound ones, both for size and the binding.

Take it everywhere with you.

- Keep it next to your bed.
- Take it into the bathroom.
- Use it to write down anything and all things related to your writing. Ideas, scraps of conversation, plots, where to send a piece next, books you'd like to read, anything.

- If you belong to this new world of smart phones, you can use your phone for this instead. Just text or email yourself the various ideas, etc.
- Then, when you have some time, not just a minute or two snatched from something else, sit down and work on your files transferring the ideas from your notebook or phone.
- OR: Flip or scroll through your notes and if you are inspired to write from some idea or plot note or bit of dialog, write!

Chapter Twenty-One

Play the title game

Still stuck for ideas or even how to get started?
Then play the title game.
It works like this: sit down with a timer set for no more than ten minutes and … start writing.
Titles.
Goofy, weird, strange, repetitious, boring, been used a million times, it doesn't matter what the titles are.
You'll be surprised at how this sparks your creativity. It's yet another way to kill the editor and let the inspiration start to flow. Once a title starts a trickle of a flood of inspiration, again, start writing.
Again this is most useful if you play and play.
I sometimes call this getting out of my own way. Instead of trying to force the writing, I use goofing around to naturally encourage the writing.

Some titles for this book: Note: I'm 5'2" tall.

> *A Short Writer Who Writes Short*
> *A Shorty Tells Tall Tales about Writing Short*
> *Short is Sweet*
> *Short Can't Be Too Sweet for Me!*

SECTION THREE

WHERE and How to Sell (MARKETS)

Chapter Twenty-Two

A-marketing we go

Nowadays, since the advent of electronic publishing, there are a plethora of markets available for submission. Some are both print and Ebook.

Here's a short list:

- **Duotrope:** https://duotrope.com: A main site to find markets of all kinds, however it does have a monthly fee, so I'd suggest using others until you have a great many short stories to sell.

- **Ralan:** http://www.ralan.com: Horror, science fiction and fantasy genres.

- **Sandra Seaman's blog, My Little Corner:** http://sandraseamans.blogspot.com: A wonderful blog focused on new short story markets.

- **The (Submissions) Grinder:** http://thegrinder.diabolicalplots.com: This is the most useful FREE site I've found for markets.

These are only a very few places to find markets.
Magazines and other markets open all the time. Many small publishers take standalone short stories too.
Make sure you go to the various market websites and read them. Look for pay rates, what they take, and what rights the publication buys.
Note that many publications buy *first time publication rights*.

What that means is that your manuscript can not have been published *anywhere before*. It varies, but some publishers consider even such things as blog and Facebook posts. Something to think about when submitting.

Exercise:

Google several word strings such as "short story markets" or be more specific and Google the genre and length of your piece and see what comes up.

- *Play* with this.
- Get comfortable with searching databases for markets.
- You'll also find specific "calls" for anthologies and magazine articles. Many of these have deadlines and other requirements, so read the guidelines carefully.

Chapter Twenty-Three

Getting paid

Start with *biggest, best paying markets*, and work your way down the list.

Trust that your work is worth money. This just makes sense, right?

In the first place, with a few exceptions, the truly "big" markets are extremely difficult to sell to.

The *New Yorker* magazine, for example, is almost impossible for an unknown, unpublished poet. I say *almost* because it's still possible. It happens … rarely.

However, consider the time and effort that it takes to submit to any market.

This doesn't mean that you should never submit to a big name market only that you should be cognizant of which markets are more accepting, welcoming, or even searching for new authors. Most of the big markets do not accept never-before-published authors or even sometimes not-yet-well-established authors.

Nowadays, there are a large number of markets that pay something, sometimes pro rates. It also makes sense to try to get paid the most you can. That's why you start with the best paying markets.

In another way to sell and get paid, I often come up with a story idea for a specific paying market or contest (more about those in the next chapter), sit down and write it and send it off. Just for fun.

Or I want to play by writing very short or in a different genre.

There are now many *very* short markets out there: Twitter magazines (140 characters or less!), six word markets, six sentences, and flash fiction, 1,000 words or less, sometimes even shorter.

These are very fun to do as an exercise.

Should you ever part with your work for FREE? No ... and yes.

There's always a lot of argument among authors about this subject.

My take? The huge majority of the time I will only sell a piece for money. This is sometimes a percentage of the royalty and free copies of the publication.

However, if it is a publication, a collection or anthology that would be great for promotional purposes then I will consider it. This is especially true if the profits are donated to charity. Several things I'm in such as *Killer Recipes*, *We'd Rather be Writing*, and *Love, Bake, Write* fit these criteria. And it was fun working with many other authors on recipes, stories and writerly advice.

Or, if I am friends with the publishers and the publication is just getting started and can't pay except in copies, I'll sometimes *donate* a piece to help out.

Two caveats:

One, watch what rights to your work you are selling.

Never, ever sell *all rights* to a short story.

All rights means the publisher owns the right to publish (whenever they choose or they may never choose to publish) your story as an Ebook, or in print, or audio, or any other way.

They also have the right to sell the story to someone else and take the money because they have all rights. Or sell the characters in your short story.

The buyer owns the rights *forever*.

If the pay is huge, you may be tempted to sell all rights. You might be thinking it's just a short story, so who cares?

Only consider: what if you want to re-sell the piece at a later time? I've done that a number of times.

Plus I've sold print or Ebook rights to one publication and then the audio rights to another.

I've also recently reprinted some of my short stories that were no longer available and I had the rights back. My *Mild West Mysteries* anthology is just one example of why you should not sell all rights.

Most publishers buy the right to publish your work one time exclusively for a period of time, in the formats they wish to publish in. For example, an anthology may be in both Ebook and print.

The period of time commonly ranges from three months to three years, depending on the publication. A few go as long as five years, which seems a bit long in my opinion. This can be another consideration when looking at markets.

The other caveat:

Never, ever pay to be published.

This is never useful for a writer. Not all the publications who request reading fees are scams—a few literary magazines come to mind—but with all the many, many places to sell, why pay?

Money goes to the author.

It is after all, your writing, *your product,* which you are selling.

Chapter Twenty-Four

It's a contest

Writing contests abound on the internet.

You can find a contest for any type, genre and length of writing, from 140 character Twitter Tweet contests to book length.

Entry fees range in price from quite expensive to free and everything in-between. Some contests award big prizes, some small and some none at all except name recognition. Some are scams and some are well regarded and some are new and some have been running for years.

So should you enter contests?

Maybe.

Depends.

There are several reasons to enter contests.

Contests, if themed, can be inspirational to your writing. Many times I've written a piece for a specific contest, submitted it and won ... something. Even if I didn't win, now I have another piece of writing that's *done*.

Woot!

Winning a contest can also be great promotion, or at the very least, some good exposure. Being an award winning author is never a bad thing with one exception: it will have no meaning if you "won" a scam contest.

Another reason to enter contests: Remember when I talked about how publishers adore already published writers? The same holds true for authors who have won a reputable and well-known contest.

Also, some contests give feedback on the entries. Depending on the experience of the editor, this can be extremely useful. After all, free editing.

So which contests should you enter? What's the criterion for entry?

It seems logical that you should enter if the contest is free and fits your writing. What have you got to lose, right?

Well, one thing you might lose is the right of first publication.

Many if not most contests publish the winners in some format. So that is a major factor to think about because remember most publishers don't take reprints.

And with some free contests you only "win the award" of First Place, Second Place or Third Place. This is fine if your piece isn't then published.

Make sure that if your piece is published you receive some form of compensation. This can be many things — gift cards, books, a cash prize, publication where you receive royalties and the list goes on and on.

I once received a cash prize, a book, some original artwork from the book, plus ... some coasters with Aboriginal designs on them. I loved the coasters.

If there is a fee only consider it if the contest is well-established, *Writers Digest*, for example. Or if it's for some other purpose, for example a conference contest for a conference you're attending or want to support.

But there are a lot of scams out there so do your research and be quite cautious of "fee" contests.

Exercise:

Find some contests on the internet.

- Research the contest to see if it inspires you to write. Or see if you have a piece that would fit as an entry.

    One way to research the contest is to look at past winners of the contest. If the winners are published on the contest's webpage, read them.

- Are the stories in the milieu that you write? Are they well written?

Other questions to ask:

- Is there a fee to enter?
- If so, what does the fee go toward? Some contests charge a fee that is then awarded to the contest winners. Sometimes conferences charge a fee for their contest to help pay for the awards.
- Is it a "real" or reputable contest? One tip: if the contest is held often, like weekly or even monthly, for a fee, it is most likely a scam.

Chapter Twenty-Five

And last, you can consider self-publishing

For several reasons self-publishing can be very useful for an author.

The first is that it is an excellent way to learn more about the publishing world and all that goes into publishing anything. Doing it yourself means you need to edit, format, get or design a cover then when it's published or about to be published you need to learn how to promote the title.

Plus, it gets your name out there. Although self-publishing — unless it sells well — is not considered a "credit" it is still effective promotion of you as an author. Perhaps for this reason, "hybrid authors," those that sell both traditionally and self-publish, are often the most successful.

Plus, you have total control over your product.

What price will your title be? You choose.

Want your title on sale? Put it on sale.

Want to change the cover? Change it.

Want to add/delete/rearrange/edit your title? Do it.

But you need to be certain that you self-publish something well-written, well-edited, and wonderful. For example, how about a reprint of a published story? But make sure you have the rights and the story is not easily found for free on the internet.

Also, consider whether you have enough "content" to be able to charge for a single story, even if it's only .99 cents.

There have been a lot of complaints on Amazon about short pieces being too short. At this time Amazon requires short pieces to be at least 2500 words long. However, that's still not very long, eight to 10 pages. So I'd suggest have a long short story or article or a collection of three plus pieces. That way you're assured of having enough content.

You might have heard of "permafree" which means permanently free. Many authors suggest this for something short to promote other titles.

However, at this time I don't suggest you try to have titles that are permafree in Ebook format.

It's difficult to do because at this time Amazon, the leader in self-published titles, doesn't easily provide a permafree option. You must make the title free on other sites such as Barnes and Noble and Smashwords first and then inform Amazon that your title can be found for less on these sites. This is because Amazon is in the business of *making money* from titles, so why have them free?

You can even have a standalone come from one of your anthologies. Just make certain that the readers know the standalone is also available in the anthology.

This works for nonfiction as well.

For example, I can copy *Section Two: The Hows* from this book and publish it as a short standalone Ebook. This is useful for those authors who want to focus only on *The Hows* of writing short. If I do this of course there will be a disclaimer mentioning that this material may also be found as a section in *Write Short to Succeed*.

Or you can combine pieces with other authors and do anthologies or collections together. This means you have more cross-promotion for the title. Consider themed anthologies or collections for even more branding of yourself as an author.

Exercise:

Go to KDP: https://kdp.amazon.com, Amazon's Ebook publishing site, and read the articles about self-publishing.

This can be a bit overwhelming at first. But remember to play with this. You're just considering self-publishing.

And remember that all the information is just that, information. Information is useful to further your success as an author.

Chapter Twenty-Six

A bonus example of what else you can do with writing short, a story *and* a recipe!

As another example of the great things you can do with writing short, here's a short story and recipe from my *The Mall Fairies Sweet Tooth Cookbook*.

Since I adore writing short stories and love to bake, I got the idea of combining two favorites into one book. Every recipe has an accompanying short story with characters from my *Mall Fairies* series.

This story has Swoop, the main character of the series, in one of her semi-heroic adventures.

SWOOP SAVES THE COOKIE LADY

Now, I don't like humans.

Overall, they're not a good thing for fairies. Overall, they're dangerous for fairies. Overall, they're fatal for fairies.

Yeah, sure, we fairies live in the attic of a shopping mall that is full of humans, but they don't know we're here. If they manage to spot us, they think we're birds or, ugh, bats.

And that includes the Cookie Lady. We sure know the Cookie Lady exists, though. Her store in the mall's Food Court is our favorite.

Or it was. A couple of weeks ago, a sign showed up in her window saying the Cookie Lady would close soon.

We fairies panicked.

No more snickerdoodles, my favorite, chocolate toffee squares or even the chocolate peanut butter no-bake oatmeal cookies? Unthinkable.

So I snuck into the air conditioning vent to spy. And while almost freezing to death, I discovered that the Cookie Lady's sales had fallen way off. The stupid humans had gotten bored with her selection. Who could get bored with snickerdoodles?

At first, I believed we were doomed to be cookie-less forever more, but then when I spotted the Cookie Lady working on the her computer and leaving it up and running, I got a great idea.

It took three hours of me surfing the internet by jumping up and down on the keys (I'm only five and a half inches tall) but I found a great new recipe for the Cookie Lady to try. I added directions for a "cookie launch" and left the printout where she'd be sure to find it.

She took the idea and added more new cookie selections including mine, and now all the fairies and humans are gaining weight from eating all her cookies.

And the Cookie Lady's store is saved!

The recipe I found follows.

CHOCOLATE WALNUT SHORTBREAD

Ingredients:

1/2 cup walnuts

1 cup white flour (Note: gluten free flours can be used, but some may burn, especially rice flour and coconut flour. Try oatmeal flour. Also reduce the heat to 300 or 275 degrees and cook longer if using a gluten free flour.)

1 stick (1/2 cup) unsalted butter, or baking margarine, or coconut oil, or ghee, room temperature, plus more for pan

1/2 cup chocolate bits (mini baking chocolate bits work best, but any chocolate is great, and the soy and dairy free chocolate bits work well)

1/4 cup powdered sugar

1 teaspoon vanilla

Preheat oven to 325 degrees.

Pulse walnuts in grinder until finely ground. Transfer to bowl, add flour and stir thoroughly.

Beat butter, sugar and vanilla until light and fluffy, add flour mix and beat until combined. Stir in chocolate bits.

Butter an 8 inch round cake pan, place dough in pan, cover with plastic wrap and press until dough is spread evenly in pan.

Cut with sharp knife into eight wedges, prick all over with fork.

Bake until golden and firm in center, 30-35 minutes. Check the shortbread often to make sure it's not burning. It can burn quickly. It's best to be a little yellow in color rather than brownish.

While still warm, recut into wedges and prick again.

Done.

VARIATIONS:

    This works well with other nuts, especially pecans. But cashews, brazil nuts and macadamia nuts may be used.

    Be sure the nuts are *unsalted and not roasted*.

    The nuts may also be omitted. However, add a ¼ to a ½ cup of butter or coconut oil or cooking margarine, plus a touch more vanilla. Otherwise the now plain shortbread with chocolate bits will be too dry and crumbly.

    You can also substitute orange extract or lemon or rum flavoring for the vanilla. I love orange with the chocolate.

Chapter Twenty-Seven

Just for fun ... and a request

Conda's note:

Here's a cautionary flash story that also ends my anthology *Mild West Mysteries: 13 Idaho Tales of Murder and Mayhem*. You might recognize an author's request within.

ENDING: READER'S CHOICE

Dora pointed at the dead woman's body slumped forward at her desk, her forehead resting on the keyboard. "I bet I know what she died of," Dora said, annoyingly answering my unspoken question.

I sighed and worked hard to tell myself that I loved being the sheriff of Starke, Idaho. Sometimes. Not right now. I rested my hand on my holster, the leather already a bit sweaty from my touch. "What are you doing here?" I asked Dora.

"Nothing. I just, um, dropped by to welcome her to Starke and found ..." Dora's chin dropped to her chest. "Oh Buddha, I hate how I keep finding dead people."

"Yup, you've got a real talent," I said and snapped my mouth shut. Where'd that yup come from? I'd better watch it or I'd be a clichéd western sheriff, chewing tobacco, wearing cowboy boots and drawling, yuck.

Time to be a regular cop.

"What do you mean you know what she died from?" I asked the one other living person in the room, Dora.

Narrowing my eyes, I studied the body. No signs of violence, unless a spilled mug of coffee, the mug emblazoned with "Writers Do It with Words," counted.

"Did you kill her?" It seemed reasonable that's why Dora would know why the writer died. Although she didn't have a single motive to murder her new neighbor that I knew of—yet.

"Me?" Dora pressed a hand to her heavy cotton, wax spattered apron. "No—I mean—well—maybe—I should have, um …"

I reached for my handcuffs at the back of my belt. Taking Dora to the station might clear her speech.

Dora must have spotted my reach, for she blurted out, "The author died from a lack of reviews of her books."

"What?"

She pointed at the computer screen, where the author's Amazon title page endlessly refreshed itself. "See? No reviews."

Ah. Now that I thought about it, I'd heard of the "review lack death phenomenon." An author's life blood is the reviews they received for their books. Without reviews, an author can wither, collapse and die.

"I read her book and was going to leave a review, but I forgot," Dora said. "So I'm partly to blame for her death." She hung her head.

Reaching out, I gently patted my friend on her shoulder. "I'm guilty too. I read her book and never got around to reviewing it."

Dora lifted her chin. "From now on, I swear to review the books I read."

I nodded, vowing to go home and review the book I'd just read. After, of course, I called the coroner, supervised the crime scene specialists, filled out the paperwork, got dinner, walked the dog and …

(And this living author thanks you for your honest review.)

Conda V. Douglas Bio and Links

Award winning author Conda grew up in the ski resort of Sun Valley, Idaho.

Her childhood was filled with authors and artists and other creative types in her parents' art gallery.

She grew up with goats in the kitchen, buffalo bones in the living room and rocks in the bathtub. Now her life is filled with her cat and dog and permanent boyfriend and writing.

She's traveled the world from Singapore to Russia — in winter! — and her own tiny office, writing all the while.

She delights in writing her cozy *Starke Dead* creative woman mystery series with amateur detective jeweler Dora Starke.

The more Dora discovers cursed jewelry, her aunt digging graves, and a rampant poisoner, the more fun Conda has — although sometimes Dora complains about her plight!

The first in the series, *Starke Naked Dead*, won Third Place in the Mystery category for the Idaho Author Awards 2014. Next up, *Starke Raving Dead*, in which Dora's mad Aunt Maddie proves the aptness of her name.

When she's not writing Dora into her quirky and quixotic mysteries, Conda writes the popular tween fantasy *Mall Fairies* series. The fairy inspiration for her *Mall Fairies* came from the sparrows that live in the Boise Towne Square Mall in Boise, Idaho.

Learn more about Conda here:

Blog: http://condascreativecenter.blogspot.com
Twitter: https://twitter.com/Conda_V
Amazon author page:
https://www.amazon.com/author/condadouglas
Pinterest: http://pinterest.com/condadouglas

www.ingramcontent.com/pod-product-compliance
Lightning Source LLC
Chambersburg PA
CBHW072014060426
42446CB00043B/2466